Does Multiple Jeopardy Exist in Mortgage Markets?

Jason Dietrich

July 2009

OCC Economics Working Paper 2009-3

Keywords: Protected Class, Discrimination, Fair Lending

Jason Dietrich is an Economist in the Compliance Risk Analysis Division at the Office of the Comptroller of the Currency. Please address correspondence to Jason Dietrich, Economist, Compliance Risk Analysis Division, Office of the Comptroller of the Currency, 250 E Street SW, Washington, DC 20219 (phone: 202-874-5119; e-mail: jason.dietrich@occ.treas.gov

Does Multiple Jeopardy Exist in Mortgage Markets?

Jason Dietrich
Office of the Comptroller of the Currency

July 2009

Abstract: Under the Home Mortgage Disclosure Act (HMDA), lenders are required to gather and report information on applicants' and coapplicants' ethnicity, race, and gender. These three characteristics are used to define protected class and control groups used for fair lending analyses. Typically, each characteristic is analyzed in isolation. This study explores whether treatment in mortgage markets is affected by belonging to multiple minority groups.

Using HMDA data from 2005 for 22 national banks, along with data from three fair lending examinations the Office of the Comptroller of the Currency (OCC) has recently conducted, we analyze whether membership of multiple minority groups is beneficial, harmful, or of no consequence to treatment in mortgage markets. Overall, there are a number of statistically and economically significant results supporting each of these effects. The primary conclusion, therefore, is that interaction effects are important and should be fully explored during fair lending analyses.

The views expressed in this paper are those of the author alone, and do not necessarily reflect those of the Office of the Comptroller of the Currency or the Department of the Treasury. The author would like to thank Ioan Voicu, John Karikari, Kostas Tzioumis, Gary Whalen, Irina Paley, Lily Chin, and Michelle Spring for their insightful comments and editorial assistance.

I. Introduction

Would a discriminatory lender treat a mortgage application from a Black male differently than an application from a Black female? Would treatment of a joint application from a Black male and White female differ from treatment of a White male and White female? How about treatment of two females versus a lone female? In each of these examples, belonging to multiple minority groups potentially affects treatment in mortgage markets. Fair lending analyses, however, typically focus on ethnic, racial, and gender effects in isolation. This creates three potential issues. First, there may be omitted variable bias if ethnic, racial, and gender effects are analyzed in isolation with no controls for the effects of the other characteristics. Second, there may be aggregation bias if treatment differs across subsets of an aggregate group. For example, focusing on the effects of all Black applicants instead of on separate effects for Black males and Black females may distort or mask underlying patterns of disparate treatment. Third, estimated disparities may not reflect the total extent of the disadvantage certain groups face. Continuing the same example, the true level of disadvantage Black females face is the sum of any disadvantage of being Black and female, as well as any additional disadvantage or interactive effect of belonging to both groups. Focusing only on one component, therefore, may not capture the total disadvantage these applicants face. In addition, from a statistical perspective, the sum of all potential effects may be significant even though the individual components are not.

This study analyzes how membership of multiple minority groups affects underwriting and pricing decisions on mortgage applications. Using 2005 Home Mortgage Disclosure Act (HMDA) data, along with data from three fair lending examinations the Office of the Comptroller of the Currency (OCC) has recently conducted, we first classify applicants into ethnic, racial, and gender groups. We then conduct a pairwise fair lending analysis of ethnic groups subset separately by race and gender, and racial groups subset by gender. This is an analysis of double jeopardy. We then extend the pairwise approach to examine the effects of membership of three or more minority groups. This is an analysis of multiple jeopardy.

This study has two objectives. First, we analyze interaction effects of group membership to determine whether belonging to multiple minority groups is harmful, beneficial, or of no consequence. If a multiplicative effect is present, an interaction effect from belonging to multiple minority groups would add a level of disadvantage to the main effects of each group. Alternatively, belonging to multiple minority groups may weaken the perceived association with any one particular group and dampen any disparate treatment. Finally, there may be no interaction effect from belonging to multiple minority groups, in which case the level of disadvantage would equal the sum of the main effects. Second, we assess the overall level of potential disadvantage faced by applicants who belong to multiple minority groups. Instead of focusing on ethnic, racial, and gender effects in isolation, this analysis examines the total potential disadvantage from belonging to each minority group separately plus any interaction effects from belonging to multiple groups.

The remainder of the paper is constructed as follows. Section II begins the discussion with background information and a brief summary of the literature. Sections III and IV present the double and multiple jeopardy analyses, respectively. Section V concludes the discussion.

II. Background

The changes to HMDA in 2004 affecting the reporting of ethnicity and race have generated much discussion on what definitions of protected class and control groups are appropriate for fair lending analyses. Most of this discussion has focused on classification strategies for ethnicity, race, and gender in isolation from the others. Correspondingly, most fair lending studies focus on estimated ethnic, racial, and gender effects in isolation from the others. This study expands the discussion to include potential interaction effects of membership in multiple minority groups.

There are three general theories about treatment of applicants from multiple minority groups.[1] The first theory is called additive multiple jeopardy.[2] In this instance, an individual who belongs to multiple minority groups receives a separate disadvantage, or main effect, from belonging to each group. However, the individual does not receive any additional disadvantage, or interaction effect, from belonging to multiple groups. The total disadvantage is simply the sum of the main effects. The second theory is called multiplicative multiple jeopardy. In this instance, in addition to main effects, there are additional interaction effects from belonging to multiple groups. The third theory suggests that belonging to multiple minority groups has a dampening effect on the overall level of discrimination.[3] If membership in multiple groups weakens the perceived association with each particular group, the level of disadvantage may be tempered. In this

---

[1] Social psychologists have extensively analyzed the effects of belonging to multiple groups. Much of this recent research is based on the crossed-categorization paradigm, which analyzes the interaction of two characteristics for two groups (Deschamps and Doise, 1978).

[2] See Berdahl and Moore (2006) for more details, particularly on additive double jeopardy.

[3] Anthropologists first observed possible reductions in bias (Evans-Pritchard, 1940).

instance, individuals receive main effects, but the interaction effects are now beneficial, thereby offsetting some of the main effects.[4]

From an empirical perspective, there is ample evidence that individuals in broad groups are not homogenous and that membership of multiple groups may affect treatment. Like most studies of discrimination, the large majority of these focused on labor markets. Berdahl and Moore (2006) show that interactions between gender and ethnicity affect treatment in labor markets. Specifically, workers who are both women and part of a minority group experience the highest level of sexual harassment at work.[5] Klawitter and Flatt (1998) provide evidence that income differs for combinations of marital status, gender, and sexual orientation. Specifically, among couples, male homosexuals have the highest incomes. At the individual level, heterosexuals have the highest incomes among males, while homosexuals have the highest income among females.[6] Ovadia (2001) analyses the interactive effects of race, class, and gender on high school seniors' values. The author finds statistically significant interactive effects between race and gender on the importance of extrinsic work characteristics, such as salary, as well as on the importance of family values. Finally, Steffensmeier, Ulmer, and Kramer (1998) show that interactions among race, gender, and age affected sentencing decisions in Pennsylvania between 1989 and 1992. Specifically, Black males ages 18–29

---

[4] In a survey of the literature, Crisp and Hewstone (1999) found that about the same number of studies showed a reduction in bias from multiple group membership as showed either no effect or a positive effect on bias. In a follow-up study, Crisp, Hewstone, and Rubin (2001) provide evidence that this dampening effect occurs only when more than two characteristics are considered.

[5] In related work, there is evidence that Black women and Latinas have lower wages on average (Browne, 1999), have the least authority in the workplace (Browne, et al., 2001; Maume, 1999), and are concentrated in the most undesirable occupations (Aldridge, 1999; Spalter-Roth and Deitch, 1999).

[6] See also Badgett (1995) and Berg and Lien (2002) for more evidence showing differential labor market outcomes for combinations of marital status, sexual orientation, and gender.

received the harshest sentences after controlling for relevant factors such as offense severity, offense type, criminal history, and various characteristics of the court. White females ages 50–69 appeared to receive the most lenient sentences.

Few studies specific to credit markets have analyzed discrimination across multiple dimensions. Robinson (2002) used data from the Boston Fed Study (Munnell et al. [1996]) to analyze differences in discrimination by race, gender, and familial status. The primary finding of this study was that White couples with children faced higher denial rates if the female partner was in the labor market as opposed to being a stay-at-home mother. The relationship for African Americans and Hispanics was exactly the opposite.

III. Double Jeopardy

This section analyzes how membership in two minority groups affects treatment in mortgage markets. It examines nine pairs of minority groups: Hispanics paired with American Indians, Asians, Blacks, Native Hawaiians, and females; and females paired with American Indians, Asians, Blacks, and Native Hawaiians.[7] We begin by focusing specifically on potential interaction effects from belonging to two minority groups. We analyze raw interaction effects using just HMDA data and then adjusted effects using data from three recent fair lending examinations. We then broaden the scope of the

---

[7] For ethnicity, individuals are categorized as Hispanic if either the primary or coapplicant reports as Hispanic. Individuals are categorized as non-Hispanic if not already categorized as Hispanic, and if either the primary or coapplicant reports as non-Hispanic. For race, individuals are categorized into a given minority group if that minority group is reported anywhere in any of the 10 HMDA racial variables. With this approach, an individual can be coded into more than one racial minority group. For individuals not coded into at least one racial minority group, if any of the five primary race variables or five coapplicant race variables convey White, the individual is then coded as White. For gender, individuals are categorized as female if either the primary or coapplicant reports as female. Individuals are categorized as male if not already categorized as female, and if either the primary or coapplicant reports as male.

analysis to assess the total disadvantage from belonging to multiple minority groups. This analysis is again conducted with both HMDA data and data from three examinations.

Interaction Effects: HMDA Data

Using HMDA data from 2005, we analyze interaction effects on underwriting decisions for first lien, one-to-four-family, owner-occupied, conventional home purchase loan applications. We do not analyze pricing disparities at this point, because pricing information in HMDA data is limited to high-cost loans. Following the OCC's approach of conducting bank-specific analyses, we conduct the analyses at the bank level. To keep the analysis manageable, we look only at the 22 largest national banks. Smaller lenders are less likely to have sufficient numbers of observations to make this type of analysis meaningful. Because HMDA data do not contain any determinants of credit decisions, the purpose of this initial analysis is to identify preliminary patterns of potential fair lending risk.

To estimate the interaction effect of membership in two minority groups, we use a logit estimator to estimate a model with a constant, two applicant characteristics, and a variable interacting the two characteristics.[8,9] For example, to estimate the interaction effect of being Hispanic and Black, the variables on the right-hand side would consist of

---

[8] Underwriting decisions are measured using a 0/1 indicator variable, where 1 denotes that the application was denied. Using the HMDA action variable, applicants with a value of 3 (denied) or 7 (preapproval denied, but Not Accepted (NA)) [[Jason: Pls define NA either as not applicable or not available.]]are coded as denials; applicants with a value of 1 (originated), 2 (approved, but NA), or 8 (preapproval approved, but NA) are coded as approvals; and applicants with a value of 4 (withdrawn), 5 (incomplete), or 6 (purchased loan) are excluded from the analysis.

[9] The minority groups include all applications that reported that minority somewhere in the application. The nonminority groups include applications that reported that group only. We ran a second set of results with the minority groups defined as applications that reported that group only. The results were basically unchanged.

a 0/1 Hispanic indicator, a 0/1 Black indicator, and a variable interacting the Hispanic and Black variables.

For continuous dependent variables, the ordinary least squares (OLS) estimate of the coefficient on the interaction variable represents the marginal effect of the interaction variable. Test statistics output by standard statistical software packages can be used to conduct hypothesis tests. This is not the case here, however, because the dependent variable is 0/1 and we use a logit estimator.[10] In this instance, the sign of the marginal effect of the interaction may differ from the sign of the estimated coefficient on the interaction variable. In addition, test statistics output by standard statistical software packages cannot be used to conduct hypothesis tests. Ai and Norton (2003) and Norton, Wang, and Ai (2004) provide the appropriate marginal effect and standard error formulations for this setup. As those two papers show, when the model includes additional independent variables, the appropriate estimated marginal effect of the interaction, as well as the appropriate estimated standard error, depend on the values of these independent variables. As a result, test statistic values vary across observations, greatly complicating interpretation of the results. Fortunately, for the model specification used in this section, where there are no independent variables other than the two indicator variables of interest along with their interaction, the estimated interaction effect and standard error are constant across observations.

Table 1 presents the results of this initial pairwise analysis based on the formulas for estimating interaction effects developed by Ai and Norton (2003) and Norton, Wang, and Ai (2004). Each row contains results for a particular bank. Each column presents the estimated interaction effects for a given pair of minority groups. For example, the first

---

[10] See Ai and Norton (2003) and Norton, Wang, and Ai (2004) for more details.

Table 1: Estimated Raw Marginal Effects of Interaction on Underwriting Decisions Using 2005 HMDA Data

	American Indian		Asian		Black		Native Hawaiian		Female
	Hispanic	Female	Hispanic	Female	Hispanic	Female	Hispanic	Female	Hispanic
Bank 1	-.1180 (.0142)	-.0293 (.0142)	-.1031 (.0173)	.0294 (.0056)	-.1330 (.0160)	.0177 (.0072)	.0126 (.0177)	-.0576 (.0181)	-.0237 (.0049)
Bank 2									
Bank 3									
Bank 4									
Bank 5						-.0332 (.0284)			-.0107 (.0255)
Bank 6									
Bank 7									-.0025 (.0120)
Bank 8				-.0027 (.0071)		.0532 (.0165)			
Bank 9						.0571 * (.0329)			
Bank 10	.0432 (.0285)	-.0081 (.0266)		.0313 (.0069)	-.0427 (.0283)	-.0143 (.0108)		.0773 (.0304)	-.0030 (.0058)
Bank 11						.0584 (.0538)			
Bank 12									
Bank 13	-.0585 (.0187)	.0285 (.0188)		.0195 (.0070)	-.0848 (.0148)	.0056 (.0053)		-.0011 (.0189)	.0062 (.0046)
Bank 14									
Bank 15									
Bank 16		-.0865 (.0714)		.0610 (.0182)		.0409 * (.0218)			-.0418 (.0207)
Bank 17									
Bank 18	-.0231 (.0370)	-.0779 (.0374)		.0093 (.0168)		-.0248 * (.0128)			.0059 (.0118)
Bank 19	-.0851 (.0115)	.0174 (.0125)	-.0629 (.0109)	.0163 (.0034)	-.1064 (.0142)	-.0102 * (.0059)	-.0151 (.0186)	.0217 (.0143)	-.0236 (.0042)
Bank 20									
Bank 21									
Bank 22	.0129 (.0326)	-.0181 (.0268)	.0140 (.0391)	-.0023 (.0102)	-.0473 (.0444)	-.0001 (.0168)	-.0620 (.0450)	-.0727 (.0349)	.0218 (.0086)

* Significant at the 90 percent level.

column of results presents the estimated interaction effects for Hispanic American Indians. As the result in the first row and column shows, being both Hispanic and American Indians lowers the raw likelihood of denial by 11.80 percent. Grey shading indicates interaction estimates that are statistically significant at the 95 percent confidence level. Grey shading with an asterisk indicates statistical significance at the 90 percent level. The negative estimates indicate that belonging to multiple groups mitigates potential discrimination. The positive estimates indicate that belonging to multiple groups exacerbates potential discrimination. Cells with no shading suggest that membership in two minority groups has no additional interaction effect. Empty cells indicate that there were insufficient numbers of applications to estimate the effects. Following OCC policy, we require at least 50 denials and approvals for each group, including the group formed by the interaction.

As table 1 indicates, feasibility is clearly an issue. For a number of pairwise analyses, there are insufficient numbers of applications to estimate the relationships. This will always be a concern when groups are analyzed at a more disaggregate level. However, in a number of cases sample sizes are sufficient. For these instances, there are two clear patterns. First, belonging to both an ethnic and racial minority appears to lessen the impact of potential disparate treatment. There are 17 results for interactions of Hispanic with a racial minority. Thirteen of these estimates are negative, while eight are negative and statistically significant. None of the four positive interaction estimates are statistically significant. The magnitudes of the negative estimates are quite high as well, ranging from –1.51 percent for Hispanic Native Hawaiians at bank 19 to –13.30 percent for Hispanic Blacks at bank 1. The results for Hispanics and Blacks are particularly strong, with all five estimates being negative and three of the five being statistically significant. Second, for Asians, and, to a lesser extent, Blacks, also being female appears to exacerbate the impact of potential disparate treatment. For Asians, six of the eight estimates are positive, and five are statistically significant. For Blacks, four of the six statistically significant effects are positive. In general, however, the magnitudes of the estimated marginal effects of interaction are smaller for race and gender pairs.

Interaction Effects: Examination Data

The previous results based on HMDA data did not account for differences in creditworthiness across applicants. Because these differences typically have a significant impact on fair lending analyses, the results in table 1 present only signals of risk. We now expand the analysis to three datasets from fair lending examinations the OCC has recently conducted. Using these data, along with the final model specifications from each examination, we again estimate interaction effects.[11] Here, we analyze interaction effects for both underwriting and pricing decisions. These results provide a much more accurate assessment of how membership in two minority groups affects treatment, because we can control for many of the legitimate factors lenders consider when underwriting and pricing loan applications.

Following up on the earlier discussion of using a logit estimator to estimate interaction effects in limited dependent variable models, the estimated interaction effects and corresponding standard errors will differ across observations when the model includes additional independent variables. Observation-dependent standard error

---

[11] The population for examinations 1 and 2 consists of applications for owner-occupied, 1-4 family, conventional loans. The population for examination 3 consists of applications for owner-occupied, 1-4 family, conventional refinance loans.

estimates are particularly problematic, because test statistics used for hypothesis testing

take on a different value for each observation. Because of these challenges associated

with the logit estimator, we instead use a linear probability estimator to estimate all

underwriting models.[12] We then use the coefficient estimate on the interaction variable as

our measure of the interaction effect. This estimate, along with the estimated standard

error, is then used to conduct hypothesis tests. These issues do not affect the pricing

analyses, because the dependent variable annual percentage rate (APR) is continuous and

we use an OLS estimator.

Tables 2 and 3 present the underwriting and pricing results, respectively. The

control variables included in each model are presented at the top of each table. The cells

of each table convey the estimated coefficient on the interaction variables. Standard

errors are included in parentheses. Grey shading denotes estimates that are and

statistically significant at the 95 percent confidence level. An asterisk indicates that the

estimate is significant at the 90 percent confidence level. Following the results from table

1, we conduct pairwise tests and report underwriting results when there are at least 50

denials and approvals from each group, including the group formed by the interaction.

For pricing, we require 50 originations per group, including the interaction group. An

empty cell conveys that insufficient applications were available to estimate the effects.

Similar to the results using HMDA data, feasibility is again an issue in some

instances. Of the available results, the patterns identified during the analysis of

underwriting decisions using HMDA data are now much weaker. In table 2, only five of

the nine ethnic/racial estimates are negative. However, four of these estimates are

_____

[12] The linear probability estimator also has shortcomings. Specifically, the errors will be hetereoskadastic, and predicted probabilities of denial may be greater than 1 or less than 0.

Table 2: Estimated Marginal Effects for Ethnic/Racial, Ethnic/Gender, and Racial/Gender Interaction Variables From Three Examinations (Underwriting Results From Linear Probability Model)

Control Variables

Examination 1: Assets, self-employed, number of major and minor derogatories, debt-to-income ratio (DTI), FICO score, lien status, term, loan-to-value ratio (LTV), loan purpose

Examination 2: Self-employed, conforming/jumbo, total derogatories, product, assets, years in current job, years in current profession, DTI, FICO score, lien status, term, LTV, loan purpose

Examination 3: Doc type, region, custom credit score, LTV, product, loan amount, property type

	American Indians		Asian		Black		Native Hawaiian		Female
	Hispanic	Female	Hispanic	Female	Hispanic	Female	Hispanic	Female	Hispanic
Exam 1	-.0430	-.0423	.0186	-.0106	.0039	-.0055	.0005	-.0031	-.0076
	(.0178)	(.0180)	(.0198)	(.0069)	(.0168)	(.0072)	(.0221)	(.0215)	(.0056)
Exam 2	-.0592	-.0034		.0052	-.0124	-.0167		.0139	-.0043
	(.0252)	(.0264)		(.0068)	(.0182)	(.0076)		(.0276)	(.0059)
Exam 3	-.0381	.0049		.0007	-.0487	.0031	.0704 *	.0529 *	-.0061
	(.0130)	(.0120)		(.0163)	(.0191)	(.0055)	(.0367)	(.0272)	(.0089)

* Significant at the 90 percent level.

statistically significant at the 95 percent confidence level. The results for Hispanic American Indians are the strongest, with all three interaction estimates showing a negative and statistically significant effect. Overall, the magnitudes of the estimates are generally smaller than the HMDA results, ranging from –5.92 percent for Hispanic American Indians for examination 2 to 7.04 percent for Hispanic Native Hawaiians for examination 3. This is typical after controlling for legitimate underwriting factors.

For the gender interactions with both ethnicity and race, only six of the 15 available estimates are positive, and only one of these is statistically significant. This contrasts with the results from table 1 showing a strong pattern of positive interactions, especially for Asians. Of the nine negative gender interaction estimates, only two are statistically significant. Therefore, for females, also belonging to an ethnic or racial minority appears to have little impact on underwriting decisions for these three lenders.

In the pricing results in table 3, there are no clear patterns. Of the nine ethnic/racial results, six are negative. Only two of these negative estimates are statistically significant at the 90 percent confidence level. Of the 14 results interacting gender with ethnicity and race, only four are positive, and only two of these are statistically significant. Alternatively, four of the 10 negative interaction effects are statistically significant. Overall, the impact of interactions is generally larger for pricing than for underwriting. The estimated effects range from –-23.43 bps for Hispanic American Indians for examination 3 to 18.33 bps for Hispanic Native Hawaiians for examination 2.

Table 3: Estimated Marginal Effects (in basis points (bps)) for Ethnic/Racial, Ethnic/Gender, and Racial/Gender Interaction Variables From Three Examinations (Pricing Results [APR] Using OLS Estimator)

Control Variables

Examination 1: Self-employed, FICO score, lien status, term, LTV, loan purpose, loan amount
Examination 2: Self-employed, FICO score, lien status, term, LTV, loan purpose, loan amount
Examination 3: Doc type, region, custom credit score, LTV, product, loan amount, property type

	American Indian		Asian		Black		Native Hawaiian		Female
	Hispanic	Female	Hispanic	Female	Hispanic	Female	Hispanic	Female	Hispanic
Exam 1	−2.53 (5.13)	−0.14 (5.57)	−3.40 (5.24)	1.96 (1.76)	−2.51 (4.95)	−2.24 (2.07)	4.97 (6.26)	−2.05 (6.21)	−6.11 (1.52)
Exam 2	.02 (5.50)	−14.42 (5.76)	−1.51 (5.21)	3.65 (1.38)	−9.81 (4.02)	−5.74 (1.67)	18.33 (6.62)	−6.49 (5.89)	9.15 (1.29)
Exam 3	−23.43 * (13.72)	−10.01 (12.52)		−6.52 (18.21)		3.28 (5.46)			−16.93 * (8.96)

* Significant at the 90 percent level.

As tables 2 and 3 show, controlling for legitimate factors that lenders consider when underwriting and pricing loans generally reduces the magnitude of the estimated interaction effects as well as the number of statistically significant effects. This is typical. However, a number of statistically significant effects still exist. During an actual fair lending examination, these findings would be examined in more detail through additional statistical tests and a review of files. Also, having only a few patterns across lenders in tables 2 and 3 is not unexpected. Given that different lenders apply different underwriting and pricing policies, there is no reason to expect that treatment of groups would be consistent across lenders.

Total Disadvantage Analysis: HMDA Data

We now broaden the perspective from an analysis of interaction effects to an analysis of the total potential disadvantage applicants from two minority groups may face. This total disadvantage consists of the sum of the main effects of belonging to each minority group plus any interaction effect from belonging to both groups. We begin with an analysis of raw effects using HMDA data. We focus only on underwriting decisions for first lien, 1-4 family, owner-occupied, conventional home purchase loan applications, and present results for the 22 largest national banks. Again, because HMDA data do not contain any determinants of credit decisions, the purpose of this initial analysis is to identify preliminary patterns of potential fair lending risk.

We focus on the difference between estimated total disadvantage and estimated main effects. This difference shows the potential error caused by focusing on main effects in isolation instead of the total disadvantage faced by applicants from multiple minority groups. To estimate total disadvantage, we use a model with 0/1 indicator variables for two groups along with an interaction variable. The model includes no other variables, and we use a logit estimator to estimate the coefficients. Using these estimates we calculate predicted probabilities of denial assuming all applicants belong to both minority groups, and then compute the average of these probabilities. We then calculate predicted probabilities of denial assuming no applicants belong to either minority group, and then compute the average of these probabilities. The difference between these two averages represents the estimated total disadvantage of belonging to both minority groups.

To estimate the main effect for a minority, we use a model with only a constant and a 0/1 variable for that group. The model includes no other variables, and we use a logit estimator to estimate the coefficients. Using these estimates we calculate predicted probabilities of denial assuming all applicants belong to the minority group, and then compute the average of these probabilities. We then calculate predicted probabilities of denial assuming no applicants belong to the minority group, and then compute the average of these probabilities. The difference between these two averages represents the estimated main effect of belonging to the minority group. Finally, we take the difference of the estimated total disadvantage and main effect.

Table 4a presents the ethnic/racial results, while table 4b presents the racial/gender and ethnic/gender results. Each row represents the results for a particular lender. The columns, which come in pairs as indicated by the double vertical lines,

Table 4a: Estimates of Total Disadvantage (Two Main Effects Plus Interaction) Less Estimated Main Effects Using 2005 HMDA

	Hispanic	American Indian	Hispanic	Asian	Hispanic	Black	Hispanic	Native Hawaiian
Bank 1	.0855	.0767	-.0315	.1486	.1095	.1185	.1530	.1844
Bank 2								
Bank 3								
Bank 4								
Bank 5								
Bank 6								
Bank 7								
Bank 8								
Bank 9								
Bank 10	.0652	.0694			.0680	.0161		
Bank 11								
Bank 12								
Bank 13	.0225	.0099			.0017	-.0220		
Bank 14								
Bank 15								
Bank 16								
Bank 17								
Bank 18	.1308	.0357						
Bank 19	.0034	.0075	-.0509	.0283	.0398	-.0139	.0341	.0647
Bank 20								
Bank 21								
Bank 22	.0159	.0171	-.0256	.0513	-.0397	-.0057	-.0065	-.0197

Table 4b: Estimates of Total Disadvantage (Two Main Effects Plus Interaction) Less Estimates of Main Effects Using 2005 HMDA

	American Indian	Female	Asian	Female	Black	Female	Native Hawaiian	Female	Hispanic	Female
Bank 1	-.0774	.1770	-.0537	.0118	-.0573	.1794	-.0839	.1303	-.0590	.1866
Bank 2										
Bank 3										
Bank 4										
Bank 5					-.0531	.1267			-.0550	.0793
Bank 6										
Bank 7										
Bank 8			-.0173	-.0001	.0013	.0963			-.0136	.0328
Bank 9					-.0265	.1238				
Bank 10	-.2046	.0305	-.0098	.0287	-.0255	.0858	.0035	.0867	-.0172	.0422
Bank 11					-.0262	.0794				
Bank 12										
Bank 13	-.0203	.0667	-.0228	.0248	-.0279	.0702	-.0301	.0239	-.0269	.0475
Bank 14										
Bank 15										
Bank 16	-.1077	.1618	-.0692	.0085	-.0748	.2967			-.1031	.1652
Bank 17										
Bank 18	-.0717	.1301	-.0346	.0499	-.0452	.0925			-.0417	.0651
Bank 19	-.0292	.0762	-.0306	-.0003	-.0386	.1246	-.0279	.0511	-.0397	.0698
Bank 20										
Bank 21										
Bank 22	-.0253	.0246	-.0169	-.0426	-.0156	.0016	-.0390	.0254	-.0123	.0388

present the estimated total disadvantage less the estimated main effect. [13] For example,

for bank 1, the value of .0855 in the first column under Hispanic suggests that the

estimated total disadvantage from being both Hispanic and American Indian is 8.55

percentage points higher than the estimated main effect of being Hispanic with no

American Indian controls. Correspondingly, for bank 1 the value of .0767 in the second

column under American Indian suggests that the estimated total disadvantage from being

both Hispanic and American Indian is 7.67 percentage points higher than the estimated

main effect of being American Indian with no Hispanic controls.

There are a number of interesting results in tables 4a and 4b. First, as with all

earlier results, feasibility is a concern, as indicated by the large number of empty cells. [14]

However, in a large number of instances volume is sufficient to estimate a set of results.

Second, the gender/race and gender/ethnicity results show a negative estimate for the

minority races and Hispanics in all but two cases (bank 8, Black, and bank 10, Native

Hawaiian). These results suggest that the total disadvantage applicants face by belonging

to a racial or ethnic minority as well as being female is actually lower than the racial and

ethnic effect estimated in isolation. In other words, estimating just main effects in these

instances overestimates the potential disadvantage. Overall, these differences are small.

However, in 13 of 40 instances, the difference is greater than 5 percent. Third, the

---

[13] Statistical hypothesis test results are not presented, because the samples for the total disadvantage and main effects analyses are not independent. As an example, suppose we are analyzing Hispanic Blacks. The sample used to estimate the total disadvantage consists of all applicants who are either Hispanic or non-Hispanic and also either Black or White. The sample used to estimate the main effect for Hispanics consists of all applicants who are either Hispanic or non-Hispanic. Similarly, the sample used to estimate the main effect for Blacks consists of all applicants who are either Black or White. Because the samples for the main effects and the total disadvantage analyses are not independent, we cannot use the standard test statistics, which assume independent samples.

[14] For underwriting analyses, we require at least 50 approvals and 50 denials for each group and also for the group defined by the interaction term. For pricing, we require at least 50 originations for each group and also for the group defined by the interaction term.

gender/race and gender/ethnicity results show a positive estimate for gender in all but three cases (banks 8, 19, and 22 for Asians). These results suggest that the total disadvantage faced by female applicants who belong to a racial or ethnic minority is higher than the female effect in isolation. In other words, estimating just main effects in these instances underestimates the potential disadvantage. Overall, these differences are large, with 23 of 40 results being greater than 5 percent. Fourth, the patterns in the racial/ethnic results are not as consistent. In general, the estimates are positive, suggesting that main effects in isolation underestimate the true level of total disadvantage. The two exceptions to this finding are the Hispanic results for the Hispanic/Asian analysis, and the Black results for the Hispanic/Black analysis. In these instances, the evidence suggests that the main effects in isolation may be overestimating the true level of total disadvantage.

Total Disadvantage: Examination Data

The previous results using HMDA data did not account for differences in creditworthiness across applicants. Because these differences typically have a significant impact on fair lending analyses, the results in tables 4a and 4b present only signals of risk. We now expand the analysis to three datasets from fair lending examinations the OCC has recently conducted. Using these data, along with the final model specifications from each examination, we again analyze total disadvantage. Here, we analyze both underwriting and pricing decisions. These results provide a much more accurate assessment of how membership in two minority groups affects treatment, since we can control for many of the legitimate factors lenders consider when underwriting and pricing loan applications.

For the underwriting analyses, we calculate the difference between estimated total disadvantage and main effects using the same process as outlined above for the HMDA analysis. For the pricing analysis, because the dependent variable is APR and an OLS estimator is used, total disadvantage is the sum of the estimated coefficients on the two minority variables plus the estimated coefficient on the interaction variable. Similarly, main effects are the estimated coefficients on the lone minority variable included in the model.

Tables 5a and 5b present the underwriting (UW) results, and tables 6a and 6b present the pricing results. The control variables for each model specification are at the top of each table. Each row represents the results for an examination. The columns, which come in pairs as indicated by the double vertical lines, present the difference in estimated total disadvantage and estimated main effect disadvantage. For example, for bank 1 the value of .0110 in the first column under Hispanic suggests that the estimated total disadvantage from being both Hispanic and American Indian is 1.10 percentage points higher than the estimated main effect of being Hispanic with no American Indian controls. Correspondingly, for bank 1 the value of –.0214 in the second column under American Indian suggests that the estimated total disadvantage from being both Hispanic and American Indian is 2.14 percentage points lower than the estimated main effect of being American Indian with no Hispanic controls.

The underwriting results in tables 5a and 5b show a number of interesting features. First, as with all earlier results, feasibility is a concern, as indicated by a number

Table 5a: Estimates of Total Disadvantage (Two Main Effects Plus Interaction) Less Estimated Main Effects From Three Examinations (UW Decisions, with Controls)

Control Variables

Examination 1: Assets, self-employed, number of major and minor derogatories, DTI, FICO score, lien status, term, LTV, loan purpose
Examination 2: Self-employed, conforming/jumbo, total derogatories, product, assets, years in current profession, DTI, FICO score, lien status, term, LTV, loan purpose
Examination 3: Doc type, region, custom credit score, LTV, product, loan amount, property type

	Hispanic	American Indian	Hispanic	Asian	Hispanic	Black	Hispanic	Native Hawaiian
Exam 1	.0110	-.0214	.0222	.0112	.0017	.0040	.0181	.0059
Exam 2	.0028	.0106			.0459	.0618		
Exam 3	-.0021	-.0135			.0227	-.0415	.0908	.0577

Table 5b: Estimates of Total Disadvantage (Two Main Effects Plus Interaction) Less Estimated Main Effects from Three Examinations (UW Decisions, with Controls)

Control Variables

Examination 1: Assets, self-employed, number of major and minor derogatories, DTI, FICO score, lien status, term, LTV, loan purpose
Examination 2: Self-employed, conforming/jumbo, total derogatories, product, assets, years in current profession, DTI, FICO score, lien status, term, LTV, loan purpose
Examination 3: Doc type, region, custom credit score, LTV, product, loan amount, property type

	American Indian	Female	Asian	Female	Black	Female	Native Hawaiian	Female	Hispanic	Female
Exam 1	-.0241	.0328	-.0139	.0215	-.0103	.0117	-.0121	.0246	-.0161	.0083
Exam 2	-.0220	.0471	-.0214	.0080	-.0238	.0373	-.0164	.0260	-.0231	.0538
Exam 3	0.126	-.0013	.0088	-.0288	.0103	.0491	.0315	.0392	.0133	-.0120

of empty cells. However, in a number of instances volume was sufficient to estimate a set of results. Second, for examinations 1 and 2, the patterns identified with HMDA data hold here. Specifically, the gender/race and gender/ethnicity results show a negative estimate for the minority races and Hispanics; the gender/race and gender/ethnicity results show a positive estimate for gender; and the patterns in the racial/ethnic results are generally positive but not very consistent. The results for examination 3 do not reflect these patterns at all. Third, not surprisingly, the magnitudes are generally small once legitimate underwriting controls are included. The largest difference is a positive estimate of 9.08 percent for Hispanics and Hispanic Native Hawaiians for examination 3.

In general, the pricing results in tables 6a and 6b are much stronger. For 35 of 46 results, the estimates are negative, suggesting that the main effects estimated in isolation are overestimating the true total disadvantage. The two exceptions are for Native Hawaiians who are also Hispanic, and females who are also black. The differences are fairly large, ranging from –29.15 bps for female American Indians for examination 3 to 18.07 bps for Hispanic Native Hawaiians for examination 2. These magnitudes suggest a significant difference between the estimated total disadvantage from belonging to multiple minority groups and the main effect of a group estimated in isolation.

IV. Multiple Jeopardy

This section expands the analysis of belonging to just two minority groups to an analysis of belonging to two or more minority groups. The first step is to define the number of minorities on the application. One approach is to extend the pairwise interaction strategy used above to interactions of three minority groups. Unfortunately,

Table 6a: Estimates of Total Disadvantage (Two Main Effects Plus Interaction) Less Estimated Main Effects (in bps) From Three Examinations (Pricing Decisions [APR], with Controls)

Control Variables

Examination 1: Self-employed, FICO score, lien status, term, LTV, loan purpose, loan amount
Examination 2: Self-employed, FICO score, lien status, term, LTV, loan purpose, loan amount
Examination 3: Doc type, region, custom credit score, LTV, product, loan amount, property type

	Hispanic	American Indian	Hispanic	Asian	Hispanic	Black	Hispanic	Native Hawaiian
Exam 1	-3.04	-3.79	-16.37	-5.98	0.25	-1.71	-3.04	1.58
Exam 2	0.98	-9.54	1.58	-13.79	-8.50	-22.35	18.07	4.42
Exam 3	-22.95	-6.91						

Table 6b: Estimates of Total Disadvantage (Two Main Effects Plus Interaction) Less Estimated Main Effects (in bps) From Three Examinations (Pricing Decisions, with Controls)

Control Variables

Examination 1: Self-employed, FICO score, lien status, term, LTV, loan purpose
Examination 2: Self-employed, FICO score, lien status, term, LTV, loan purpose, loan amount
Examination 3: Doc type, region, custom credit score, LTV, product, loan amount, property type

	American Indian	Female	Asian	Female	Black	Female	Native Hawaiian	Female	Hispanic	Female
Exam 1	-6.25	-1.07	-6.25	-12.21	-4.11	2.28	-6.55	-6.74	-8.05	-3.61
Exam 2	-7.46	-3.94	-2.91	5.47	-5.81	1.05	-5.12	1.53	-2.87	-9.86
Exam 3	-9.82	-29.15	-8.28	-9.80	-3.62	9.95			-10.92	-14.21

the cell sizes of these interaction terms get small very quickly, so this is not a feasible strategy. Instead, we use three different raw count measures. The first measure counts the number of different racial minorities reported in the application. Here, multiple occurrences of the same group are ignored. For example, if both the primary and coapplicant report Black, this adds only one to the measure. Because there are four possible racial minorities in HMDA, this measure takes on values from 0 to 4. The second measure counts the number of racial, ethnic, and gender minorities reported in the application. Again, multiple occurrences of the same group are ignored. This measure is just the first measure plus ethnicity and gender, so it takes on values from 0 to 6. The third measure counts the total number of occurrences of any minority group in any of the primary and coapplicant ethnicity, racial, and gender variables. Here, multiple occurrences of the same group are counted separately. HMDA, has two ethnic variables, 10 racial variables, and two gender variables. Both ethnicity variables and both gender variables could convey a minority group. Since there are only four racial minorities, only four of the primary applicant racial variables and four of the coapplicant racial variables could convey a minority group. Therefore, this measure takes on values from 0 to 12 (= 2 + 2 + 8).[15]

Using these three measures, we analyze the relationship between the number of minorities reported in mortgage applications and the underwriting and pricing decisions. Similar to the double jeopardy analysis, we begin by analyzing patterns in underwriting decisions using the 2005 HMDA data for the 22 largest national banks. We then extend

_____

[15] For each of these measures, the specific composition of the application is ignored. For example, using the first measure, an application from a single Black applicant and an application from a single Asian applicant would both have a value of 1. Allowing composition to matter is not feasible owing to the large number of possible unique combinations for the ethnic, racial, and gender variables and the subsequent sample-size problems.

the analysis to both underwriting and pricing decisions for three fair lending examinations the OCC recently conducted.

HMDA Data

To begin the multiple jeopardy analysis, we again examine underwriting decisions using 2005 HMDA data. We measure underwriting decisions using a 0/1 indicator variable, where 1 denotes the application was denied. For each measure of the number of minorities, we compute the denial rates for each possible value of those count measures. The analysis includes only denial rates based on 30 or more applications.

Graphs 1–3 present all the results. Graph 1 shows the denial rate for each value of the racial minority count variable. We compute denial rates separately by bank, so there is a separate graph for each bank. Bank 2 did not meet the sample-size requirement, so that graph is excluded. Because this analysis examines the effects of belonging to multiple minority groups, the focus is not how denial rates change going from zero minorities to one minority. Instead, the focus is on how denial rates change going from one to two minorities, from two to three minorities, and from three to four minorities.

One of the first items of note in graph 1 is limitations on the feasibility of this analysis. No banks had more than 30 applications with three or four racial minorities, and only seven had at least 30 applications with two minorities. For five of these seven banks (banks 1, 10, 18, 19, and 22), the denial rate was higher for applications with two minorities than applications with one minority. These differences ranged from 5 percent

Graph 1: Percentage Denied by Number of Racial Minorities on the Application, by Lender

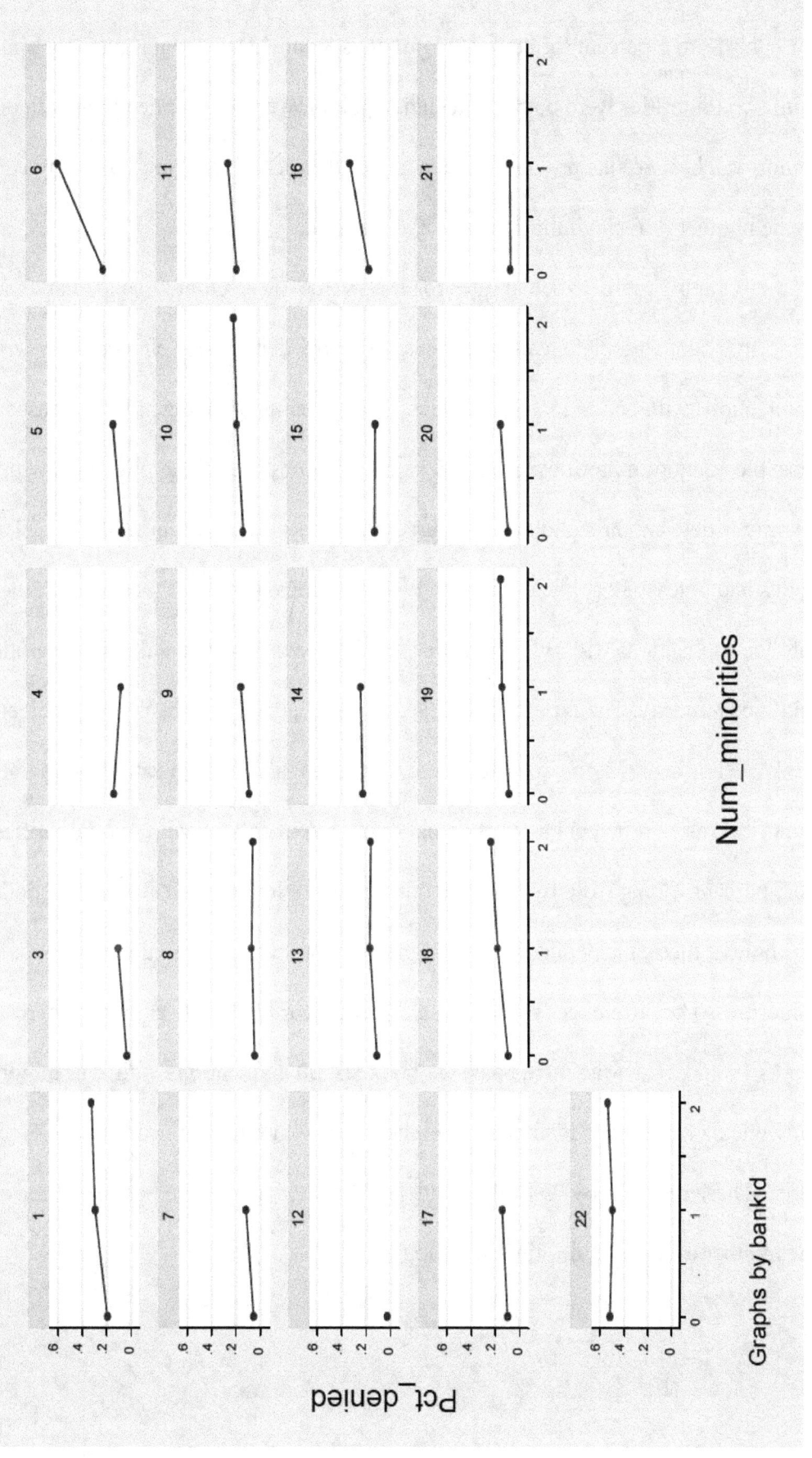

for bank 18 to 1 percent for bank 19. For banks 8 and 13, the denial rates for applications with two minorities were both 1 percentage point lower than applications with one minority. These results provide some evidence that denial rates are positively correlated to the number of racial minorities on an application.

Graph 2 presents denial rates for each value of the ethnic, racial, and gender minority count variable. Again, the focus is on how denial rates change across groups of applications with one or more minorities. Adding ethnicity and gender increases the possible count of minorities to six. No banks had more than 30 applications with five or six minorities, but three did have at least 30 applications with four minorities. Twenty banks had at least 30 applications with two minorities. For 19 of these banks, the denial rate for applications with two minorities was higher than the denial rate for applications with one minority. The differences ranged from 25 percent for bank 6 to 1 percent for bank 21. For bank 22, the one exception, the denial rate for applications with one minority was 51.4 percent and the denial rate for applications with two minorities was 50.7 percent. Going from two to three minorities, 12 lenders had at least 30 applications. For nine of these, the denial rate was higher for applications with three as opposed to two minorities. The differences ranged from 7 percent for bank 1 to less than 1 percent for banks 19 and 21. Of the three banks with at least 30 applications with four minorities, only one had a higher denial rate for applications with four minorities as opposed to three. These results provide further evidence that denial rates are positively correlated to the number of racial minorities on an application.

Graph 2: Percentage Denied by Number of Ethnic, Racial, and Gender Minorities on the Application, by Lender

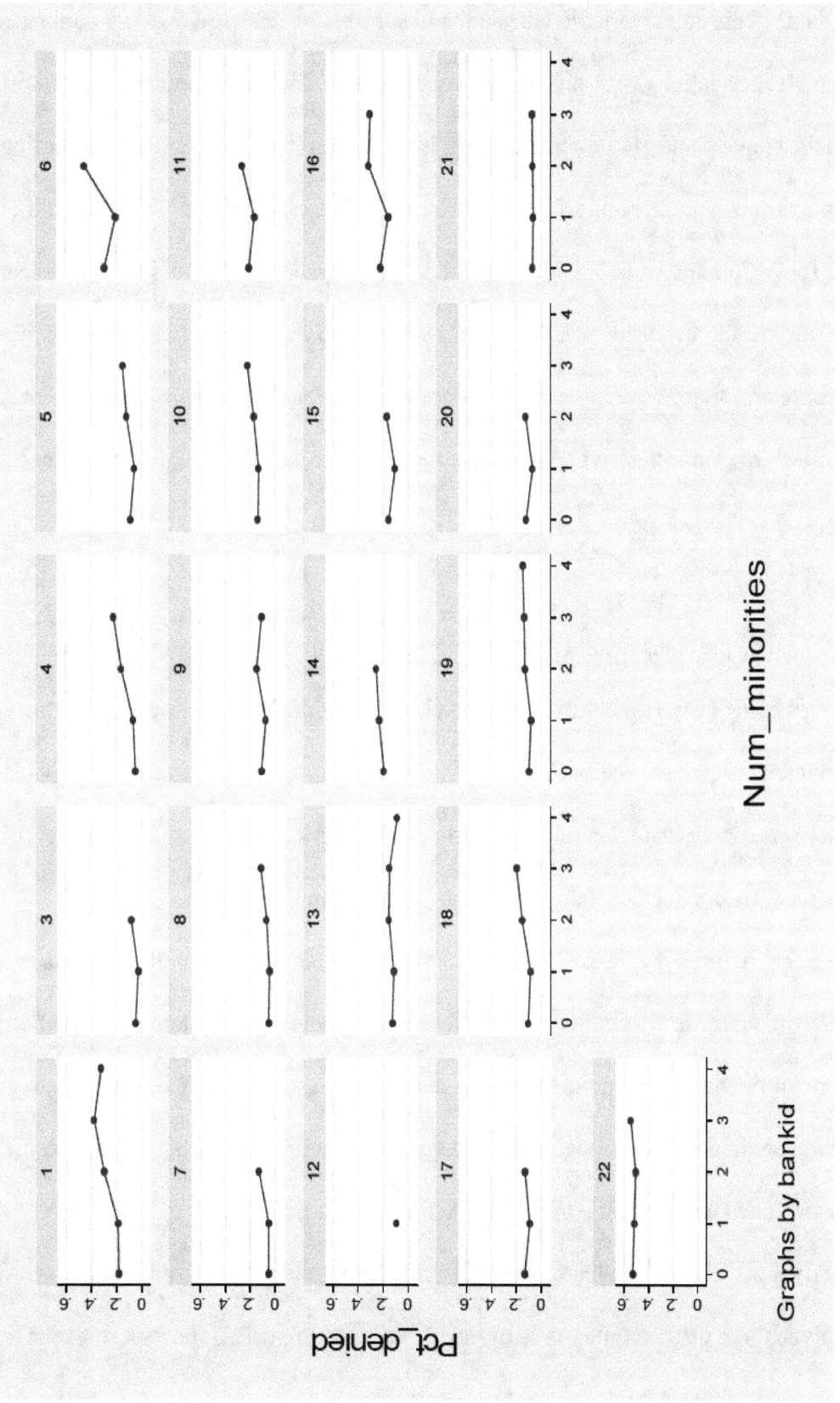

Graph 3 presents denial rates for each value of the total possible minority count variable. This count variable takes on values from 0 to 12. However, no banks had more than 30 applications with seven or more minorities. The largest number of minorities was six for banks 1 and 19. In general, there is an upward trend in denial rates starting from applications with one minority. The three possible exceptions are banks 13 and 19, which are fairly flat, and bank 8, which has an inverted U-shape. Bank 1 shows the clearest upward trend, increasing steadily from 18.5 percent for applications with one minority to 50 percent for applications with six minorities. Again, these results suggest that higher numbers of minorities on applications are positively correlated with denial rates.

Examination Data

The previous results presented the effects of belonging to multiple minority groups using only HMDA data with no controls for differences in creditworthiness across applicants. Because creditworthiness typically has a significant impact on any test of discrimination, we now employ data from three fair lending examinations that the OCC has recently conducted. Using these data, along with the final model specifications from the examinations, we again analyze the effects of belonging to multiple minority groups. To estimate these effects, we construct a set of 0/1 indicator variables representing each value of the particular minority count measure being analyzed. We then include these 0/1 indicators in the model specification from each examination, with "zero minorities" as the excluded category. We then analyze the relative magnitudes of the estimated coefficients on these indicator variables. Following the results from graphs 1–3, we analyze three different measures of the number of minorities, and report results

Graph 3: Percentage Denied by Total Number of Minorities on the Application, by Lender

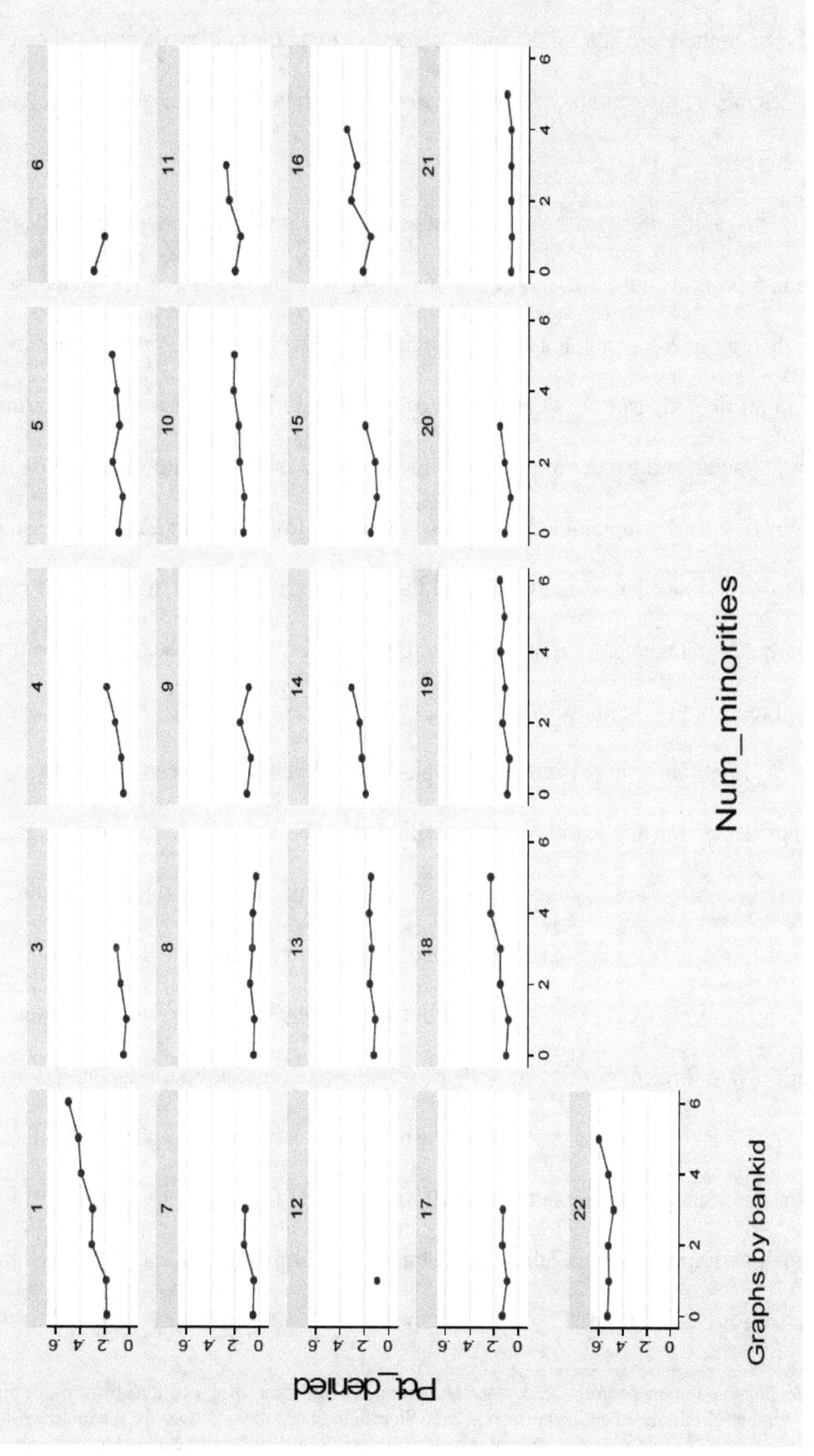

Num_minorities

Graphs by bankid

only when there are at least 50 approvals and denials for underwriting or 50 originations for pricing. These sample-size criteria apply to each indicator variable for the count measures.

Graph 4 presents the coefficient estimates from the underwriting analysis, and graph 5 presents the coefficient estimates from the pricing analysis. In each case, there are three graphs for each lender, corresponding to the three different measures of number of minorities. Measure 1 is the number of racial minorities; measure 2 is the number of ethnic, racial, and gender minorities; and measure 3 is the total number of possible minorities. Each graph includes results with no control variables and results using the control variables that were used during the actual examination. Unlike earlier graphs where the first data point represented zero minorities, for all these graphs, the first data point represents one minority.

In graph 4, there is generally a positive correlation between the number of minorities on the application and the likelihood of being denied.[16] In all nine graphs, when no controls are included, the coefficient estimate for applications with two minorities is higher than the coefficient estimate for applications with only one minority. Adding controls weakens this pattern, but five graphs still show a similar result. Going from two to three minorities shows a positive impact in examinations 1 and 2 using the ethnic, racial, and gender measure (measure 2), but a negative impact in all other instances. Similarly, for examinations 1 and 2, going from three to four minorities shows a positive impact on the likelihood of denial for examinations 1 and 2, but a negative impact for examination 3.

---

[16] Each data point on the graph represents the estimated coefficient for a 0/1 indicator variable representing the number of minorities on the horizontal axis. Since a logit estimator is used for the underwriting analyses, only the relative magnitude of the estimates is relevant, and not the actual magnitudes.

Graph 4: Relationship Between Number of Minorities and Denial Rates for Three Examinations

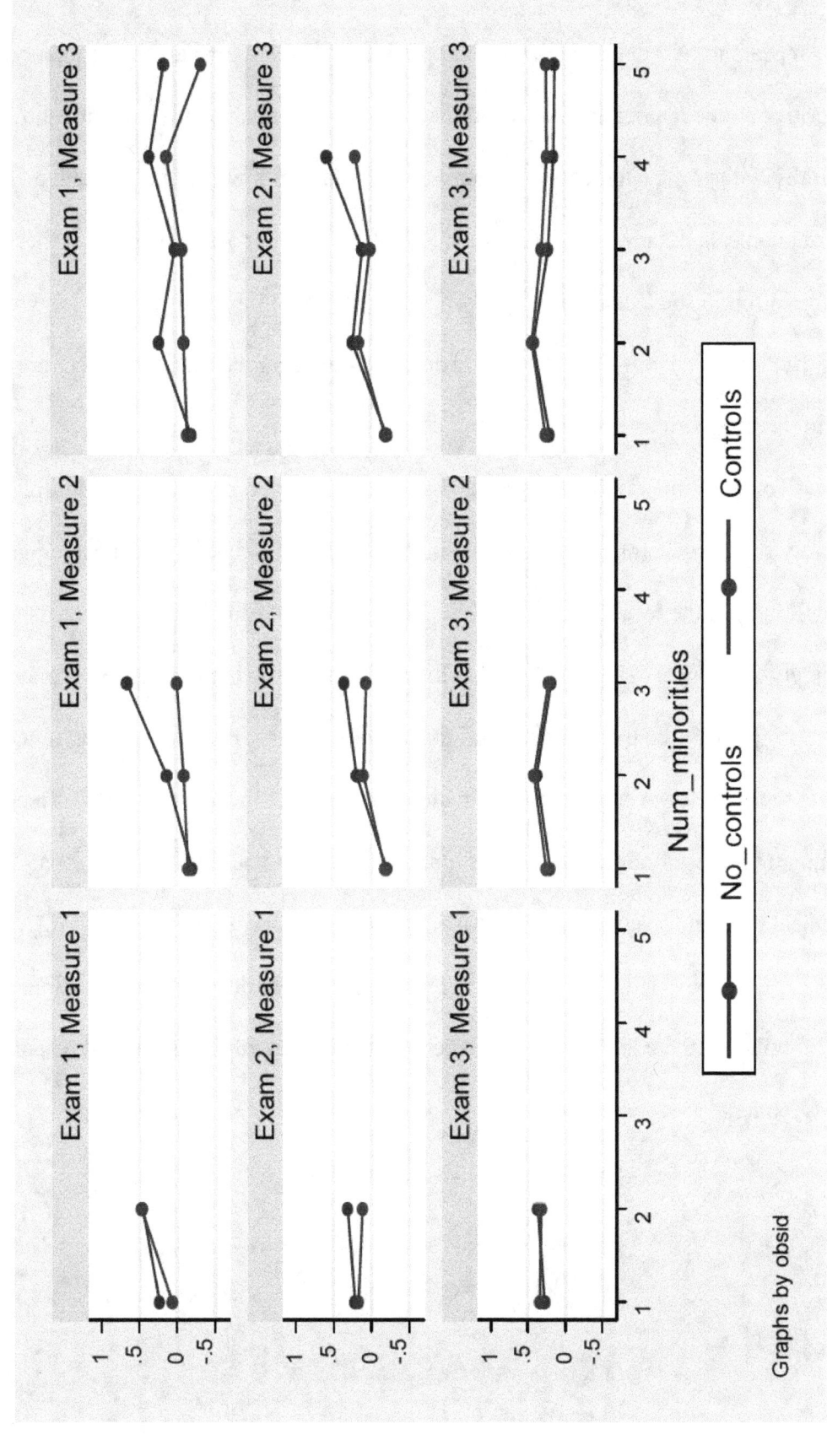

Graphs by obsid

In graph 5, the results are just the opposite of the underwriting results. In general, there appears to be a negative relationship between APR (in bps) and the number of minorities on the application. For examinations 1 and 2, this negative relationship generally holds for each measure of number of minorities and for models with and without controls. Exam 3 is an exception to this pattern. For the two broadest measures of number of minorities, there is a slightly positive effect going from applications with one minority to applications with two minorities, and then a strong negative effect going from two to three minorities.

Together, the findings in graphs 4 and 5 suggest that belonging to multiple minority groups generally increases the likelihood of denial but lowers the average APR paid. Similar to the results for double jeopardy, controlling for legitimate factors lenders consider when underwriting and pricing loans significantly dampened the estimated relationships between the number of minorities and underwriting and pricing outcomes. This is typical. However, a number of patterns still exist. During an actual fair lending examination, these finding would be examined in more detail through additional statistical tests and a review of files. Also, the lack of patterns across lenders in graphs 4 and 5 is not unexpected. Given that different lenders apply different underwriting and pricing policies, there is no reason to expect that treatment of groups would be consistent across lenders.

Graph 5: Relationship Between Number of Minorities and APR (bps) for Three Examinations

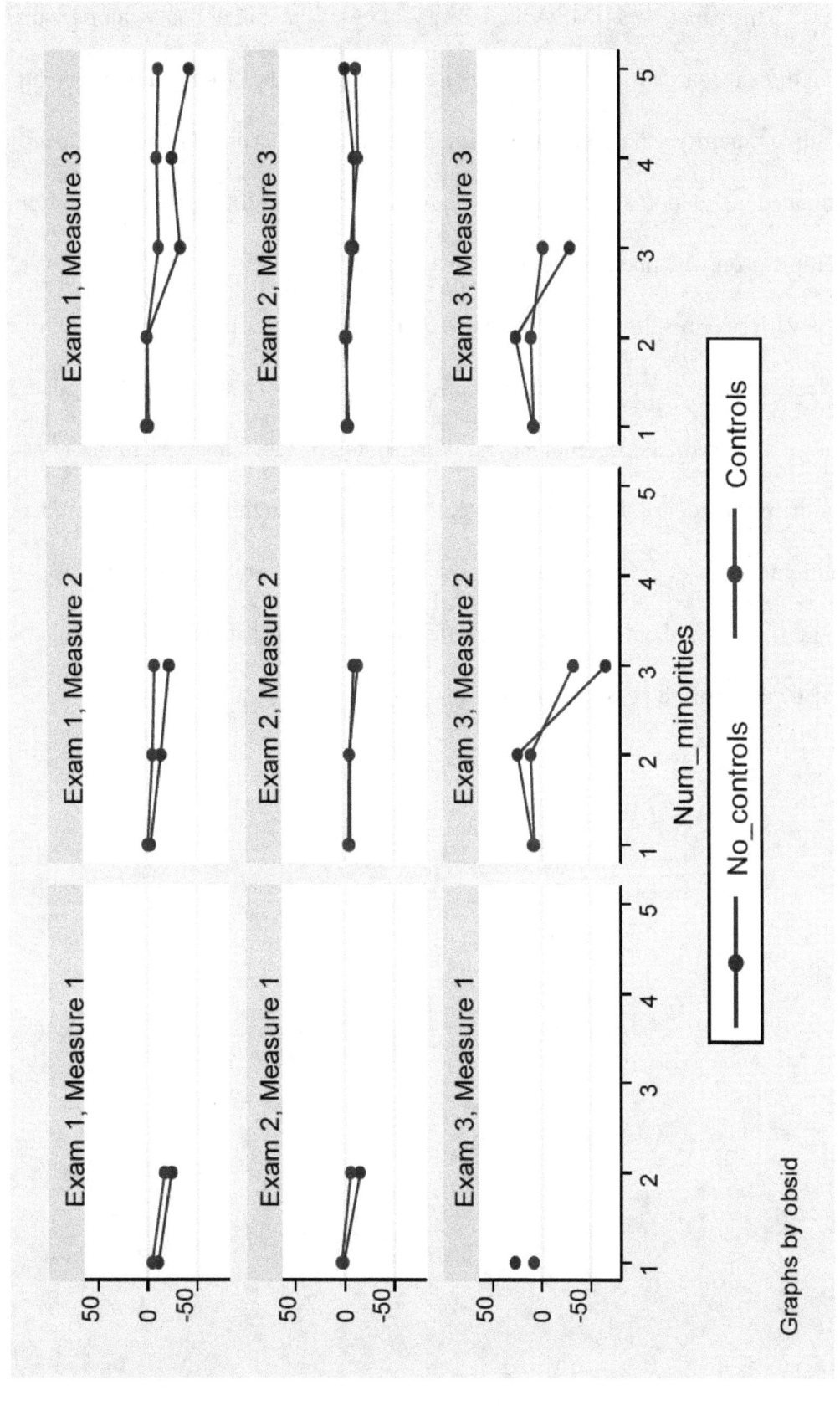

Graphs by obsid

V. Conclusion

This paper uses HMDA data from 2005 for 22 national banks, along with data from three recent fair lending examinations, to analyze the effects of membership in multiple minority groups on underwriting and pricing decisions. It focuses specifically on estimated interaction effects and also on how estimates of total disadvantage from multiple group membership compare to estimated main effects in isolation. Overall, a wide variety of results support basically every perspective. There is no reason to expect all lenders to treat applicants similarly, so this diversity of results is not surprising, given that we analyzed 25 different lenders. What should be taken away from these results is that there is evidence for most of the lenders examined in this study that membership in multiple groups does have an effect on underwriting and pricing decisions. Therefore, fair lending analyses should test for these effects and, if such effects are found, additional statistical work and possible a review of files should be conducted.

References

Ai, Chunrong, and Edward C. Norton. 2003. Interaction Terms in Logit and Probit Models." *Economics Letters* 80:123–29.

Aldridge, D. 1999. Black Women and the New World Order: Toward a Fit in the Economic Marketplace. In *Latinas and African American Women at Work: Race, Gender and Economic Inequality,* edited by I. Browne, 357–79. New York: Russell Sage Foundation.

Badgett, M. V. L. 1995. The Wage Effects of Sexual Orientation Discrimination. *Industrial and Labor Relations Review* 48 (4):726–39.

Berdahl, Jennifer L., and Celia Moore. 2006. Workplace Harassment: Double Jeopardy for Minority Women. *Journal of Applied Psychology* 91 (2): 426–36.

Berg, Nathan, and Donald Lien. 2002. Measuring the Effect of Sexual Orientation on Income: Evidence of Discrimination? *Contemporary Economic Policy* 20 (4):394–414.

Browne, I., ed. 1999. *Latinas and African American Women at Work: Race, Gender and Economic Inequality.* New York: Russell Sage Foundation.

Browne, I., C. Hewitt, L. Tigges, and G. Green. 2001. Why Does Job Segregation Lead to Wage Inequality Among African Americans? Person, Place, Sector, or Skills? *Social Science Research* 30:473–95.

Crisp, Richard J., and Miles Hewstone. 1999. Differential Evaluation of Crossed Category Groups: Patterns, Processes, and Reducing Intergroup Bias. *Group Processes and Intergroup Relations* 2:307–33.

Crisp, Richard J., Miles Hewstone, and Mark Rubin. 2001. Does Multiple Categorization Reduce Intergroup Bias? *Personality and Social Psychology Bulletin* 27 (1):76–89.

Deschamps, J. C., and W. Doise. 1978. Crossed Category Memberships in Intergroup Relations. In *Differentiation Between Social Groups,* edited by H. Tajfel, 141–58. Cambridge, UK: Cambridge University Press.

Evans-Pritchard, E. E. 1940. *The Nuer.* London: Oxford University Press.

Klawitter, M. M., and V. Flatt. 1998. The Effects of State and Local Antidiscrimination Policies on Earnings for Gays and Lesbians. *Journal of Policy Analysis and Management* 17 (4):658–86.

Maume, D. J., Jr. 1999. Glass Ceilings and Glass Escalators: Occupational Segregation and Race and Sex Differences in Managerial Promotions. *Work and Occupations* 26:483–509.

Munnell, Alicia H., Lynn E. Browne, James McEneaney, and Geoffrey M.B. Tootell. (1996). Mortgage Lending in Boston: Interpreting HMDA Data. *American Economic Review,* 86(1): 25-53.

Norton, Edward C., Hua Wang, and Chunrong Ai. 2004. Computing Interaction Effects and Standard Errors in Logit and Probit Models. *The Stata Journal* 4 (2):154–67.

Ovadia, Seth. 2001. Race, Class, and Gender Differences in High School Seniors' Values: Applying Intersection Theory in Empirical Analysis. *Social Science Quarterly* 82 (2):340–56.

Robinson, Judith K. 2002. Race, Gender, and Familial Status: Discrimination in One US Mortgage Lending Market. *Feminist Economics* 8 (2):63–85.

Spalter-Roth, R., and C. Deitch. 1999. I Don't Feel Right Sized: I Feel Out Sized: Gender, Race, Ethnicity, and the Unequal Costs of Displacement. *Work and Occupations* 26:446–82.

Steffensmeier, Darrell, Jeffery Ulmer, and John Kramer. 1998. The Interaction of Race, Gender, and Age in Criminal Sentencing: The Punishment Cost of Being Young, Black, and Male. *Criminology* 36 (4):763–97.